Swoop, Creep and Cling

by Cara Torrance

OXFORD
UNIVERSITY PRESS
AUSTRALIA & NEW ZEALAND

Looking for Food

Hawks swoop, chipmunks dart and black panthers run. Frogfish creep and sea stars cling to rocks. This is how they look for food.

Claws, jaws and teeth help them eat.

Hawks

Hawks can see well. This helps them look for food in the day. When hawks see food, they swoop down.

This hawk saw a bird and swoops to pursue it.

Hawks eat insects and birds. Their beak and claws help them eat.

beak

claw

Chipmunks

Chipmunks run on the ground. They dart about from tree to tree, looking for food.

Chipmunks eat nuts and seeds.

Chipmunks pick up food with their paws. They eat with their sharp teeth. They keep some food in **cheek pouches**.

cheek pouch

Black Panthers

Black panthers hunt at night. They lie in wait, then leap out at their **target**.

paw

Black panthers have strong teeth and jaws to help them eat.

sharp teeth

Frogfish

Frogfish lie still, then creep on their fins when food comes near. They draw fish to them with a **lure** on their **dorsal fin**.

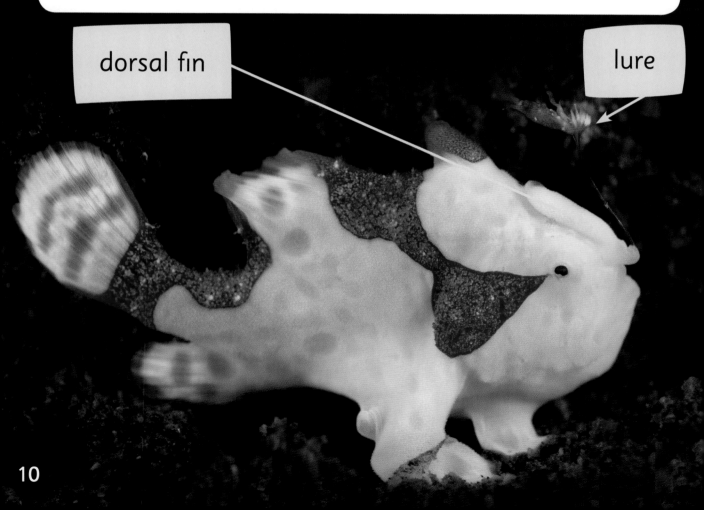

dorsal fin

lure

Frogfish eat by sucking fish into their big mouth.

mouth

Sea Stars

Sea stars have lots of legs. Their legs have little cups that can form a kind of glue. The glue helps sea stars stick to rocks and grip food.

cup

Sea stars eat oysters. They suck the food from the shell.

Oysters are food for sea stars and people.

	How it looks for food	How it eats food
Hawk	Sees well from the air	beak, claws
Chipmunk	Looks on the ground and in trees	teeth, cheek pouches
Black panther	Hunts at night	claws, teeth
Frogfish	Lure and big mouth	jaws, mouth
Sea star	Legs and feet with glue	mouth

Look It Up

cheek pouches: pockets between the jaw and cheeks to keep food in

dorsal fin: a fin on the top of a fish

lure: part of a fin that draws fish near

target: the thing you are aiming to get

Index